Smithsonian

DINOSAURS

Coloring Book

ILLUSTRATED BY
Rachel Curtis

IDW

Facebook: **facebook.com/idwpublishing**
Twitter: **@idwpublishing**
YouTube: **youtube.com/idwpublishing**
Instagram: **@idwpublishing**

ISBN : 978-1-68405-819-8   22 23 24 25   6 5 4 3

TEXT BY
**NATIONAL MUSEUM OF
NATURAL HISTORY**

ILLUSTRATIONS BY
RACHEL CURTIS

EDITED BY
JUSTIN EISINGER

EDITORIAL ASSISTANCE BY
**ALONZO SIMON,
ZAC BOONE AND
JENNIFER EISINGER**

DESIGNED BY
RICHARD SHEINAUS
FOR **GOTHAM DESIGN**

IDW Publishing does not read or accept unsolicited submissions of ideas, stories, or artwork. For international rights, contact licensing@idwpublishing.com

Nachie Marsham, Publisher
Blake Kobashigawa, SVP Sales, Marketing & Strategy
Mark Doyle, VP Creative & Editorial Strategy
Tara McCrillis, VP Publishing Operations
Anna Morrow, VP Marketing & Publicity
Alex Hargett, VP Sales
Jamie S. Rich, Executive Editorial Director
Scott Dunbier, Director, Special Projects
Greg Gustin, Sr. Director, Content Strategy
Kevin Schwoer, Sr. Director of Talent Relations
Lauren LePera, Sr. Managing Editor

Keith Davidsen, Director, Marketing & PR
Topher Alford, Sr. Digital Marketing Manager
Patrick O'Connell, Sr. Manager, Direct Market Sales
Shauna Monteforte, Sr. Director of Manufacturing Operations
Greg Foreman, Director DTC Sales & Operations
Nathan Widick, Director of Design
Neil Uyetake, Sr. Art Director, Design & Production
Shawn Lee, Art Director, Design & Production
Jack Rivera, Art Director, Marketing

Ted Adams and Robbie Robbins, IDW Founders

Special thanks to the team at the Smithsonian for all of their assistance and support.

Smithsonian Enterprises:
Kealy Gordon, Product Development Manager
Jill Corcoran, Director, Licensed Publishing
Janet Archer, DMM, Ecom and D-to-C
Carol LeBlanc, President

National Museum of Natural History:
Matthew T. Miller, Museum Specialist, Department of Paleobiology
Michelle Pinsdorf, Fossil Preparator

Established in 1846, the Smithsonian is the world's largest museum and research complex, dedicated to public education, national service, and scholarship in the arts, sciences, and history. It includes 19 museums and galleries and the National Zoological Park. The total number of artifacts, works of art, and specimens in the Smithsonian's collection is estimated at 156 million. The Department of Paleobiology at Smithsonian's National Museum of Natural History is home to over 40 million specimens, representing fossil invertebrates, vertebrates, and plants from all over the world.

CAMARASAURUS

PRONUNCIATION: KAM-aer-a-SORE-us

NAME MEANING: Chambered lizard, because of the air-filled sacs in its vertebrae to lighten them

SIZE: ~15 - 23 m (49 - 75 ft) long

WEIGHT: ~45,350 kg (100,000 lbs)

TIME PERIOD: Late Jurassic period (156 - 146 mya)

ENVIRONMENT: Open fern forests of western North America

DIETARY STRATEGY: Herbivory

KEY TRAIT(S): Long neck, spoon-shaped teeth

Known for its long neck that could reach into the tree ferns of its day, *Camarasaurus* was among the most common sauropod dinosaurs in a world filled with giants. *Camarasaurus* shared its environment with at least 10 other giant sauropod (long-necked) dinosaur species. *Camarasaurus* had large, spoon-shaped teeth it used to pull coarse plant material from trees. These teeth could not chew; the giant sauropods swallowed the vegetation whole. Unlike many other dinosaurs, the giant sauropods did not care for their children. Once the egg was laid, the *Camarasaurus* juvenile was on its own.

CAMPTOSAURUS

PRONUNCIATION: KAMP-toh-SORE-us

NAME MEANING: Bent flexible lizard, for the flexibility of the back vertebrae

SIZE: ~6 - 8 m (20 - 26 ft) long

WEIGHT: ~900 - 1,000 kg (2,000 - 2,200 lbs)

TIME PERIOD: Late Jurassic period (156 - 146 mya)

ENVIRONMENT: Open fern forests of western North America

DIETARY STRATEGY: Herbivory

KEY TRAIT(S): Bird-hipped (ornithischian) dinosaur, could walk on two legs or four

*C*amptosaurus used four legs for walking, but could stand on its hind legs to reach leaves in trees or to run quickly for short distances. They are thought to have cared for their young. They lived at the same time as *Camarasaurus*, *Stegosaurs*, *Diplodocus*, *Allosaurus*, and a host of other dinosaur species.

ALLOSAURUS

PRONUNCIATION: AL-oh-SORE-us

NAME MEANING: Different lizard, because its neck bones looked different from the neck bones of other dinosaurs

SIZE: ~9 - 10 m (28 - 32 ft) long

WEIGHT: ~1,800 kg (4,000 lbs)

TIME PERIOD: Late Jurassic period (156 - 146 mya)

ENVIRONMENT: Open fern forests of western North America

DIETARY STRATEGY: Carnivory

KEY TRAIT(S): Short horns above the eyes, three-fingered hands

This fearsome hunter was one of the most common big predators of the Late Jurassic. *Allosaurus* had a strongly built skull with 80 serrated teeth that were continually replaced, so they never got a chance to wear out or lose their edge. Its large jaw could open a massive 79 degrees. Above each eye it had a narrow horn. *Allosaurus* used its strong back legs to run and its long tail for balance as it chased herds of plant-eating animals. Three hooked claws at the end of its fingers measured 18 cm (7 in.) long.

EUOPLOCEPHALUS

PRONUNCIATION: yoo-OP-loh-SEF-a-lus

NAME MEANING: True armored head, due to the bony plates that cover the head

SIZE: ~5.5 - 7 m (18 - 23 ft) long

WEIGHT: ~2,500 kg (5,600 lbs)

TIME PERIOD: Late Cretaceous (76.4 - 75.6 mya)

ENVIRONMENT: Coastal plains and deltas of western North America

DIETARY STRATEGY: Herbivory

KEY TRAIT(S): Armored back and head, bony sledgehammer-like tail

The massive-jawed tyrannosaurids that prowled Late Cretaceous North America were often no match for armored dinosaurs like *Euoplocephalus*, with its hammer-like tail that could swing sideways with leg-shattering force. It had hundreds of small bony nodules across its back that formed a shield, a broad hornlike beak with small teeth for slicing fibrous plants, and a large digestive system for long slow processing of coarse plant material. Its wide skull was covered with small interlocking bony plates. Even the eyelids were armored with small, bony shutters. A complex system of nasal passages filled its bulbous snout.

MASIAKASAURUS

PRONUNCIATION: ma-SHEEK-a-SORE-us

NAME MEANING: Vicious lizard, from the Malagasy word *masiaka*

SIZE: ~2 m (6 - 7 ft) long

WEIGHT: ~20 - 45 kg (44 - 100 lbs)

TIME PERIOD: Late Cretaceous (70 - 66 mya)

ENVIRONMENT: Semi-arid coastal plains with wet and dry seasons of Madagascar

DIETARY STRATEGY: Carnivory

KEY TRAIT(S): Forward-projecting front teeth

*M*asiakasaurus was a small bipedal theropod dinosaur with distinctive forward-projecting teeth. These teeth were likely adapted for catching small prey animals, such as early mammals and small reptiles. *Masiakasaurus* lived on the island of Madagascar, which by this time was already isolated from neighboring continents.

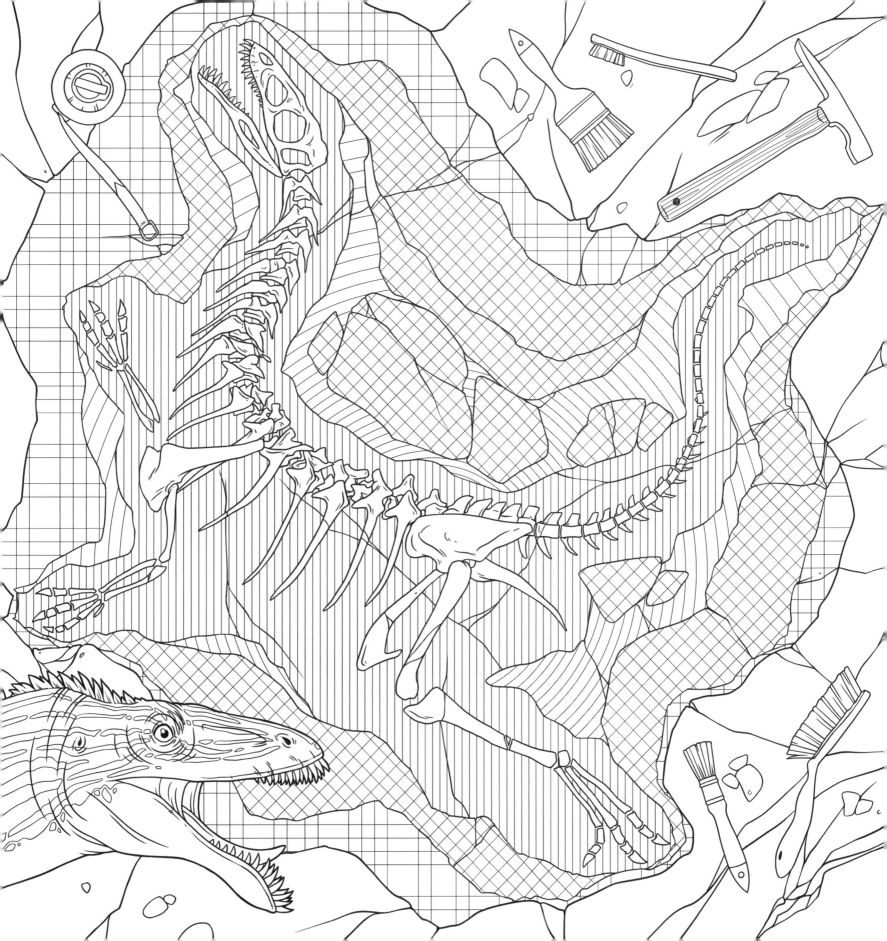

MAJUNGASAURUS

PRONUNCIATION: ma-JUNG-a-SORE-us

NAME MEANING: Majunga lizard, after the Mahajanga Province of Madagascar in which it was found

SIZE: ~5.5 - 8 m (18 - 26 ft) long

WEIGHT: ~1,100 - 1,400 kg (2,400 - 3,000 lbs)

TIME PERIOD: Late Cretaceous (70 - 66 mya)

ENVIRONMENT: Semi-arid coastal plains with wet and dry seasons of Madagascar

DIETARY STRATEGY: Carnivory

KEY TRAIT(S): Blunt snout, very small forelimbs with no finger claws

*M*ajungasaurus' short snout is thought to be an adaptation not unlike those of big cats, to hold struggling large prey animals. It was the largest predator on Madagascar and was capable of killing the large sauropods on the island. The forelimb was short but very strong and robust. It was likely reduced to account for the immense weight of the skull as in other large meat-eating dinosaurs.

STEGOCERAS

PRONUNCIATION: stehg-AH-SER-us

NAME MEANING: Horn roof, after the little horns that surround the skull rim

SIZE: ~2 - 2.5 m (6 - 8 ft) long

WEIGHT: ~10 - 40 kg (22 - 88 lbs)

TIME PERIOD: Late Cretaceous (77.5 - 74 mya)

ENVIRONMENT: Coastal plains and deltas of western North America

DIETARY STRATEGY: Herbivory

KEY TRAIT(S): Dense, domed skull surrounded by small horns, or tubercles

S*tegoceras* is a small member of the pachycephalosaur family of dinosaurs. Numerous skulls have been found, and they show a remarkable growth series from babies to adults. Juveniles had very flattened heads, while the dome became more pronounced as the animals aged. The dome has been suggested to be for head-butting behaviors or sexual display.

THERIZINOSAURUS

PRONUNCIATION: ther-ih-ZEEN-oh-SORE-us

NAME MEANING: Scythe lizard, after the large 1 m (3.3 ft) long claws on its hands

SIZE: ~9 - 10 m (30 - 33 ft) long

WEIGHT: ~3,600 - 5,000 kg (8,000 - 11,000 lbs)

TIME PERIOD: Late Cretaceous (70 - 68 mya)

ENVIRONMENT: Dense forests of Mongolia

DIETARY STRATEGY: Herbivory

KEY TRAIT(S): Each hand was armed with three 1 m (3.3 ft) long claws

*T*herizinosaurus had arms that were equipped with long feathers, much like wings, and feathered skin. Its long bony tail may have been adorned with feathery plumes. The *Therizinosaurus* had strong hind legs for standing, like all known theropods, and its bulky body contained the large digestive system of a plant eater. It was amazingly tall, possibly for reaching into treetops, and defended itself with incredibly long, sickle-like claws.

TYRANNOSAURUS

PRONUNCIATION: TIE-ran-oh-SORE-us

NAME MEANING: Tyrant lizard, due to its large size and perceived dominance over other species

SIZE: ~9 - 12 m (30 - 40 ft) long

WEIGHT: ~8,000 - 14,000 kg (18,000 - 30,000 lbs)

TIME PERIOD: Late Cretaceous (68 - 66 mya)

ENVIRONMENT: Coastal forests or swamps of western North America

DIETARY STRATEGY: Carnivory

KEY TRAIT(S): Large head with very reduced, two-fingered forelimbs

Around the age of 13, *Tyrannosaurus* had a growth spurt that added almost 2 kg (5 lbs) a day for four years. This predator could easily travel long distances on its long hind limbs. Like birds of today, the *Tyrannosaurus* walked on its toes, each with a pointed claw that provided a steady foothold. The stiff tail helped this large dinosaur balance its heavy head, which contained a large brain that allowed it to quickly process information about its surroundings. *Tyrannosaurus* had a huge olfactory lobe in its brain, giving it an amazing sense of smell, with which it could find prey or dead carcasses.

UTAHRAPTOR

PRONUNCIATION: yoo-TAW-rap-TOR

NAME MEANING: Thief of Utah, after the state in which it was found in the United States

SIZE: ~4.5 - 7 m (15 - 23 ft) long

WEIGHT: ~270 - 500 kg (600 - 1,100 lbs)

TIME PERIOD: Early Cretaceous (139 - 135 mya)

ENVIRONMENT: Coastal forests and floodplains of western North America

DIETARY STRATEGY: Carnivory

KEY TRAIT(S): Large claw on the second toe

*U*tahraptor is the largest known member of the raptor family. At over 2 m (6 ft) tall it would have looked like a very large bird with its feathered-covered body and wing-like feathers on its hands. *Utahraptor* fossils have been found in clusters which strongly suggests that they hunted in family groups. The large claw on the toe was likely for holding down struggling prey or used like a climbing hook to stay on large herbivores during an attack.

EORAPTOR

PRONUNCIATION: EE-oh-rap-TOR

NAME MEANING: Dawn thief, meaning thief from the beginning of the age of dinosaurs or the "dawn"

SIZE: ~1 m (3 ft) long

WEIGHT: ~10 kg (22 lbs)

TIME PERIOD: Late Triassic (231 - 228 mya)

ENVIRONMENT: Humid floodplains of Argentina

DIETARY STRATEGY: Omnivory

KEY TRAIT(S): Small, light, and agile

One of the earliest dinosaurs known, *Eoraptor* was no bigger than a fox, and possibly with a similar way of life. Its diet was lizards, small reptiles, and plants. It had all-purpose teeth, most of which are curved, pointed blades suitable for eating meat. But the teeth at the front of the jaw had broader crowns, and are those of plant eaters. So it's likely the *Eoraptor* ate both plants and animals. The eyes on the side of the head enabled all-around vision. It stood on three strong toes, but had a fourth toe at the back of the foot. *Eoraptor* had a long neck, typical of the saurischian group of dinosaurs, and scaly skin like most reptiles. Its long tail helped it balance as it ran on its hind legs.

EORAPTOR SKULL
ACTUAL SIZE

CERATOSAURUS

PRONUNCIATION: ser-AT-oh-SORE-us

NAME MEANING: Horn lizard, after the prominent horn on the snout and two smaller horns above the eyes

SIZE: ~5 - 7 m (17 - 23 ft) long

WEIGHT: ~450 - 680 kg (1,000 - 1,500 lbs)

TIME PERIOD: Late Jurassic period (156 - 146 mya)

ENVIRONMENT: Open fern forests of western North America, Europe and Africa

DIETARY STRATEGY: Carnivory

KEY TRAIT(S): The prominent horns on the head

*C*eratosaurus had ostoderms running down the middle of the neck, back, and tail. These were small bones embedded in the skin, similar to those seen in crocodiles today. Analysis of the *Ceratosaurus* brain reveals this dinosaur had a good sense of smell. Its fossils are often found in association with *Allosaurus*, and the two animals probably often competed for prey. It is unlikely that the two fought very often, as *Allosaurus* is significantly larger, which would have kept *Ceratosaurus* at bay. The fingers of *Ceratosaurus* were much shorter than in other theropods and were likely not very good at grasping prey. *Ceratosaurus'* horns were likely used for display only.

SUCHOMIMUS

PRONUNCIATION: soo-K-oh-MIME-us

NAME MEANING: Crocodile mimic, owing to the shape of the skull resembling a crocodile's

SIZE: ~9.5 - 11 m (31 - 36 ft) long

WEIGHT: ~1,800 - 4,500 kg (4,000 - 10,000 lbs)

TIME PERIOD: Early Cretaceous (125 - 112 mya)

ENVIRONMENT: Tropical floodplains of north Africa

DIETARY STRATEGY: Piscivory (fish-eating)

KEY TRAIT(S): Crocodile-like snout, teeth adapted for grasping instead of slicing

A member of the spinosaurus family, *Suchomimus* used its narrow snout and crocodile-like teeth to catch fish. It likely waded into ponds, lakes, and rivers waiting for fish to swim by, like a modern heron. It had taller-than-normal vertebrae, which gave it a low sail-like structure along its back.

ACROCANTHOSAURUS

PRONUNCIATION: ak-ro-KANTH-oh-SORE-us

NAME MEANING: High-spined lizard, after the prominently tall vertebrae that form a low sail-like structure

SIZE: ~11.5 m (38 ft) long

WEIGHT: ~7,250 kg (16,000 lbs)

TIME PERIOD: Early Cretaceous (116 - 110 mya)

ENVIRONMENT: Coastal floodplains and open forests of western North America

DIETARY STRATEGY: Carnivory

KEY TRAIT(S): Tall ridge along the back

Known from only three individual skeletons, *Acrocanthosaurus* is thought to have been the apex predator of its day. Its most prominent feature was the tall vertebrae that formed a ridge along the back. The vertebrae were attached to powerful muscles that helped *Acrocanthosaurus* balance its body, and may have had other unknown functions. Though their backs looked similar, *Acrocanthosaurus* was not related to *Suchomimus*. Instead, *Acrocanthosaurus* was closely related to *Allosaurus*. Much like *Allosaurus*, *Acrocanthosaurus* probably fed on the large sauropods with which it shared its surroundings.

PLATEOSAURUS

PRONUNCIATION: PLATE-ee-oh-SORE-us
NAME MEANING: Broad lizard, due to its robust limb bones
SIZE: ~5 - 10 m (16 - 33 ft) long
WEIGHT: ~600 - 4,000 kg (1,300 - 8,800 lbs)
TIME PERIOD: Late Triassic (214 - 204 mya)
ENVIRONMENT: Forests and swamps of central Europe
DIETARY STRATEGY: Herbivory
KEY TRAIT(S): Long flexible neck

*P*lateosaurus was one of the largest dinosaurs of its period, likely able to walk on either two or four legs. Its long bendy neck allowed it to reach for nutritious leaves in tall trees. This early relative of the sauropods sliced and chopped plant material with serrated, cone-shaped teeth at the front of its jaw and leaf-shaped teeth at the back. *Plateosaurus* most likely had birdlike lungs which supplied a lot of oxygen quickly, fueling fast growth and movement. Its arms were strong with large claws, perhaps used to grasp food or for fighting as well as walking. Robust legs gave *Plateosaurus* the power to run on two legs while a long strong tail, flexible and packed with muscle, helped provide balance.

COELOPHYSIS

PRONUNCIATION: SEE-low-FYE-sis

NAME MEANING: Hollow form, referencing the numerous air chambers in their vertebrae

SIZE: ~2.5 - 3 m (8 - 10 ft) long

WEIGHT: ~15 - 20 kg (33 - 44 lbs)

TIME PERIOD: Late Triassic – Early Jurassic (216 - 196 mya)

ENVIRONMENT: Arid desert plains with seasonal lakes and riverbeds of North America and Africa

DIETARY STRATEGY: Carnivory

KEY TRAIT(S): A long flexible neck allowed Coelophysis to turn its jaws in any direction

The small *Coelophysis* was one of the earliest-known theropods to roam the planet. This lightweight hunter was a fast and active predator that traveled in a pack and likely fed on small reptiles and other creatures. It had serrated teeth that angled back like barbed hooks, making them ideal for catching prey, which it swallowed whole. The *Coelophysis* may have hunted in family groups so the young could learn from their parents. It had tough skin that was probably covered by an outer layer of small protective scales.

STAURIKOSAURUS

PRONUNCIATION: STORE-ee-koh-SORE-us

NAME MEANING: Southern Cross lizard, after the prominent constellation in the southern hemisphere

SIZE: ~2.25 m (7.5 ft) long

WEIGHT: ~30 kg (66 lbs)

TIME PERIOD: Late Triassic (233 mya)

ENVIRONMENT: Deserts of South America

DIETARY STRATEGY: Carnivory

KEY TRAIT(S): Boxy head and long, grasping claws

One of the earliest known dinosaurs, *Staurikosaurus* is known from just a few fragmentary skeletons. Its teeth are all serrated and curved, suggesting a carnivorous diet, and the relatively long arms were likely very good at catching small prey animals. It is considered to be the most primitive dinosaur.

PSITTACOSAURUS

PRONUNCIATION: SIT-ack-oh-SORE-us
NAME MEANING: Parrot lizard, after the shape of its beak
SIZE: ~1.5 - 2 m (5 - 7 ft) long
WEIGHT: ~13.5 - 20 kg (30 - 45 lbs)
TIME PERIOD: Early Cretaceous (126 - 101 mya)
ENVIRONMENT: Wooded forests of east Asia
DIETARY STRATEGY: Herbivory
KEY TRAIT(S): Parrotlike beak

A small dinosaur that resembled a parrot, *Psittacosaurus* came complete with a beak and quills. This plant eater was a common forest dweller in Early Cretaceous Asia. An early relative of the *Triceratops*, it used its beak to slice off vegetation, which would have been shredded by its small, sharp teeth. Tail quills may have been related to the feathers of today's birds, though very distantly. Prominent horns on the cheeks grew with age, which suggests they might have been used for attracting a mate. *Psittacosaurus* may have been capable of complex behaviors, such as caring for their young, as evidenced by a specimen found next to 34 hatchlings. Many *Psittacosaurus* specimens have been unearthed, ranging from tiny babies to full-grown adults.

STYRACOSAURUS

PRONUNCIATION: sti-RAK-oh-SORE-us

NAME MEANING: Spiked lizard, after the large spikes on the frill

SIZE: ~4.5 - 6 m (15 - 20 ft) long

WEIGHT: ~2,500 kg (5,500 lbs)

TIME PERIOD: Late Cretaceous (75.5 - 75 mya)

ENVIRONMENT: Coastal swamps and floodplains of western North America

DIETARY STRATEGY: Herbivory

KEY TRAIT(S): Spiked frill at the back of its head

*S*tyracosaurus was a herd dinosaur with jaws built to chew up the plants it ate. Like other ceratopsians, *Styracosaurus* had a narrow, hooked beak like that of a parrot, for selecting the most nutritious foods. This ceratopsian had a big frill crown with long spikes. Its bony frill had large gaps in it to keep it light, making it strong as well as impressive. *Styracosaurus* also had a long horn at the top of its nose, like a rhinoceros. These spikes and horn likely served both to provide protection and attract mates.

PACHYRHINOSAURUS

PRONUNCIATION: pack-E-rhino-SORE-us

NAME MEANING: Thick-nosed lizard, due to its thick, bony snout

SIZE: ~6 - 8 m (20 - 26 ft) long

WEIGHT: ~2,000 - 2,700 kg (4,500 - 6,000 lbs)

TIME PERIOD: Late Cretaceous (73.5 - 68.5 mya)

ENVIRONMENT: Coastal floodplains and swamps of western North America

DIETARY STRATEGY: Herbivory

KEY TRAIT(S): Thick snout

Like other ceratopsians, the *Pachyrhinosaurus* jaw contained hundreds of teeth for chewing plants. Instead of horns, their skulls had massive flattened bony areas over the nose and eyes. This may have supported a hornlike covering made of keratin, similar to that of the modern musk ox. *Pachyrhinosaurus* would have used these for defense, and for combat with other members of its species. It lived in herds which it would have needed for protection against the large members of the Tyrannosaur family that were the dominant predators of its age.

APATOSAURUS

PRONUNCIATION: ah-PAT-oh-SORE-us

NAME MEANING: Deceptive lizard, owing to the unusual shape of certain bones in the tail that did not look like those of other dinosaurs

SIZE: ~21 - 23 m (69 - 75 ft) long

WEIGHT: ~16,000 - 22,000 kg (36,000 - 48,000 lbs)

TIME PERIOD: Late Jurassic (152 - 151 mya)

ENVIRONMENT: Open fern forests of western North America

DIETARY STRATEGY: Herbivory

KEY TRAIT(S): Long neck and large size

Though scientists once believed the *Apatosaurus* to have a very flexible neck, now we know these dinosaurs and their relatives held their necks out very straight in front of the body. They would use their necks to reach plants in high places, moving their mouths side to side as they ate, only taking a step after they had gobbled up all the plants. *Apatosaurus* had eggs that were the size of basketballs. That is tiny compared to a full-grown sauropod. *Apatosaurus* is the proper scientific name for "Brontosaurus," which was discarded as a proper scientific name almost a century ago.

DREADNOUGHTUS

PRONUNCIATION: dred-NAWT-us

NAME MEANING: Fears nothing, owing to the animal's immense size rendering adult individuals impervious to attack

SIZE: ~26 m (85 ft) long

WEIGHT: ~22,000 - 38,000 kg (48,000 - 84,000 lbs)

TIME PERIOD: Late Cretaceous (75 mya)

ENVIRONMENT: Floodplains and coastal forests of South America

DIETARY STRATEGY: Herbivory

KEY TRAIT(S): Unusually long neck, even for a sauropod

Known from just two skeletons, *Dreadnoughtus* is estimated to be the heaviest land animal yet discovered. Its neck was almost 12.2 m (40 ft) long, and it would have stood over 6 m (20 ft) tall at the shoulder. The excavated skeletons of *Dreadnoughtus* belonged to dinosaurs that had not reached maturity. The adult animals were likely even larger. The two skeletons were found together, having died in a flash flood.

ARCHAEOPTERYX

PRONUNCIATION: ar-kee-OP-ter-ix
NAME MEANING: Old wing
SIZE: ~50 cm (20 in.) long
WEIGHT: ~.8 - 1 kg (1.8 - 2 lbs)
TIME PERIOD: Late Jurassic (151 - 148 mya)
ENVIRONMENT: Dry woodlands
Diet**DIETARY STRATEGY:** Carnivory
KEY TRAIT(S): The oldest known bird, *Archaeopteryx* had a bony tail, clawed wings, and toothed jaw

A feathered dinosaur that could fly, the crow-sized *Archaeopteryx* shared many traits with common birds. Unlike a modern bird, *Archaeopteryx* had heavily toothed jaws, claws on its wings, and a long bony tail. It was very similar to many of the feathered but flightless theropod dinosaurs found recently in China, except its wings were longer and the wing feathers were the same basic shape as those of flying birds. While it is possible *Archaeopteryx* could fly, it probably could not fly very well. This would make it the earliest known flying dinosaur, but scientists still cannot agree if it can really be called a bird.

TROODON

PRONUNCIATION: TROH-eh-don

NAME MEANING: Wounding tooth, due to the heavy serrations on its teeth

SIZE: ~2.3 m (7.5 ft)

WEIGHT: ~14 - 23 kg (30 - 50 lbs)

TIME PERIOD: Late Cretaceous (77.5 - 76.5 mya)

ENVIRONMENT: Floodplains, swamps, and coastal forests of western North America

DIETARY STRATEGY: Carnivory

KEY TRAIT(S): Coarsely serrated teeth, prominent feathers, large eyes

Small, birdlike dinosaurs, *Troodon* and its relatives had the largest brain-to-body size ratio of any dinosaur. Their large eyes provided stereoscopic vision, allowing them to hone in on prey, even at night. They had feather-covered, grasping hands to help grab small prey animals like mammals, reptiles, and smaller dinosaurs.

TRICERATOPS

PRONUNCIATION: try-SER-a-tops
NAME MEANING: Three-horned face
SIZE: ~7.6 - 9 m (25 - 30 ft) long
WEIGHT: ~9,070 - 12,000 kg (20,000 - 26,500 lbs)
TIME PERIOD: Late Cretaceous (68 - 66 mya)
ENVIRONMENT: Subtropical floodplains of western North America
DIETARY STRATEGY: Herbivory
KEY TRAIT(S): Large skull with three horns and bony frill

*T*riceratops was the biggest of the horned dinosaurs. The spectacular skull of the *Triceratops* is one of the biggest known among fossilized dinosaur skulls, up to 2.4 m (8 ft) long. It had three horns with sharp tips and strong bony cores, and a giant frill at the back of its head. It may have used its horns in battle against other *Triceratops*. This dinosaur had a sharp parrotlike beak. The *Triceratops* had closely packed rows of teeth that were continuously shed and replaced throughout its life, able to slice through plant foods like scissors.

EDMONTOSAURUS

PRONUNCIATION: ed-MONT-oh-SORE-us

NAME MEANING: Lizard from Edmonton, after the city in Canada near where it was first found

SIZE: ~12 - 15 m (39 - 49 ft) long

WEIGHT: ~4,500 - 9,000 kg (10,000 - 20,000 lbs)

TIME PERIOD: Late Cretaceous (73 - 66 mya)

ENVIRONMENT: Subtropical floodplains of western North America

DIETARY STRATEGY: Herbivory

KEY TRAIT(S): Multiple rows of cheek teeth formed broad, ridged grinding surfaces in each jaw

Equipped with a sharp beak and some of the most efficient chewing teeth that have ever evolved, *Edmontosaurus* was one of the most successful plant eaters of the Late Cretaceous. The hadrosaurs, or duck-billed dinosaurs, were among the most specialized of the ornithopods. They were named for the duck-like beak, which varied in shape depending on their diet. *Edmontosaurus* was one of the biggest, and had an unusually broad beak suitable for gathering a lot of food at once without stopping to pick and choose. Its bulky body contained a large digestive system that could deal with anything it ate, especially when the food had been chewed to pulp by millstone-like teeth.

IGUANODON

PRONUNCIATION: ig-WAH-no-don
NAME MEANING: Iguana tooth
SIZE: ~10 m (33 ft) long
WEIGHT: up to 4,080 kg (9,000 lbs)
TIME PERIOD: Early Cretaceous (126 - 122 mya)
ENVIRONMENT: Swamps and forests of Europe
DIETARY STRATEGY: Herbivory
KEY TRAIT(S): Could stand up and run on its hind legs—useful for both intimidation and escaping danger; thumb spike.

The *Iguanodon* was a plant eater with iguana-like teeth, from which it gets it name. Leaf-shaped teeth are typical of the early plant-eating dinosaurs. The animal used them to chew plants gathered with its sharp beak, made of hard keratin. The Iguanodon had joined fingers: the three middle fingers were bound together with flesh, and the thumb was a hardened spike. The skull was tall and quite narrow, providing the animal with high-set eyes that gave it a wide field of vision. The *Iguanodon* used its padded hands to walk on the ground. The *Iguanodon* was covered with tough skin that protected it from infections and scratches.

PARASAUROLOPHUS

PRONUNCIATION: para-SORE-oh-LOAF-us

NAME MEANING: Near-crested lizard, in reference to another duck-billed dinosaur *Saurolophus*

SIZE: ~9.5 m (31 ft) long

WEIGHT: ~2,250 - 2,700 kg (5,000 - 6,000 lbs)

TIME PERIOD: Late Cretaceous (76.5 - 73 mya)

ENVIRONMENT: Coastal swamps and floodplains of western North America

DIETARY STRATEGY: Herbivory

KEY TRAIT(S): Large, tube-like crest on the head that arched back over the neck

The *Parasaurolophus* had strong arms that allowed it to walk on all fours when looking for food. Its legs had powerful muscles attached to big, strongly-built hip bones, while a long heavy tail helped the dinosaur balance on its hind legs. The *Parasaurolophus* had a tough beak, sharp-edged and broad, perfect for gathering plant food. It also had a high back, with tall extensions of the spine bones that made its back much higher than usual. The impressive bony crest of this elegant plant eater contained a network of tubes that extended throughout the nasal passage, like a bony version of an elephant's trunk. The tubes probably worked like a trumpet to generate very loud, booming calls that may have helped the animals stay in contact in dense forests.

OURANOSAURUS

PRONUNCIATION: ooh-RAN-oh-SORE-us

NAME MEANING: Courageous lizard

SIZE: ~7 - 8.3 m (23 - 27 ft) long

WEIGHT: ~2,700 - 3,600 kg (6,000 - 8,000 lbs)

TIME PERIOD: Early Cretaceous (113 - 125 mya)

ENVIRONMENT: Floodplains and sub-tropical forests

DIETARY STRATEGY: Herbivory

KEY TRAIT(S): Tall "sail" ridge on its back

*O*uranosaurus was a plant eater with an unusual skeleton, featuring a large head and long jaws. It had a horny beak on the front of its long snout. A large sail on its back may have helped in maintaining its body temperature or in mating displays. This tall, defining structure was supported by bony extensions of its backbone.

THESCELOSAURUS

PRONUNCIATION: THESS-kel-oh-SORE-us

NAME MEANING: Wondrous lizard

SIZE: ~2.5 - 4 m (8 - 13 ft) long

WEIGHT: ~200 - 300 kg (450 - 660 lbs)

TIME PERIOD: Late Cretaceous (68 - 66 mya)

ENVIRONMENT: Coastal forests and floodplains of western North America

DIETARY STRATEGY: Herbivory or Omnivory

KEY TRAIT(S): Sharp beak, small hands, robust hind limbs

*T*hescelosaurus stood on stocky hind legs and was likely a swift runner. Its front teeth were sharp and pointed while its back teeth were leaf-shaped. *Thescelosaurus* likely possessed coloring that would help it blend in with surroundings to avoid predators.

HESPERORNIS

PRONUNCIATION: hess-PER-ORN-is

NAME MEANING: Western bird, as it was found in western North America

SIZE: ~1.5 - 1.8 m (5 - 6 ft) long

WEIGHT: ~9 - 18 kg (20 - 40 lbs)

TIME PERIOD: Late Cretaceous (83.5 - 78 mya)

ENVIRONMENT: Shallow seas of western North America and Asia

DIETARY STRATEGY: Piscivory (fish-eating)

KEY TRAIT(S): Toothed beak, very reduced arms, large webbed feet

With a similar appearance to a large cormorant, *Hesperornis* was a bird, and therefore, a dinosaur. *Hesperornis* likely spent most of its life at sea, diving to catch fish and squid and returning to the surface to breathe and to sleep. Its large webbed feet could propel it very fast through the water, while its long flexible neck helped it catch prey. Its beak had dozens of needle-like teeth, good for catching slippery fish. *Hesperornis* fragments have been found in the stomachs of large aquatic reptiles called *mosasaurs*.

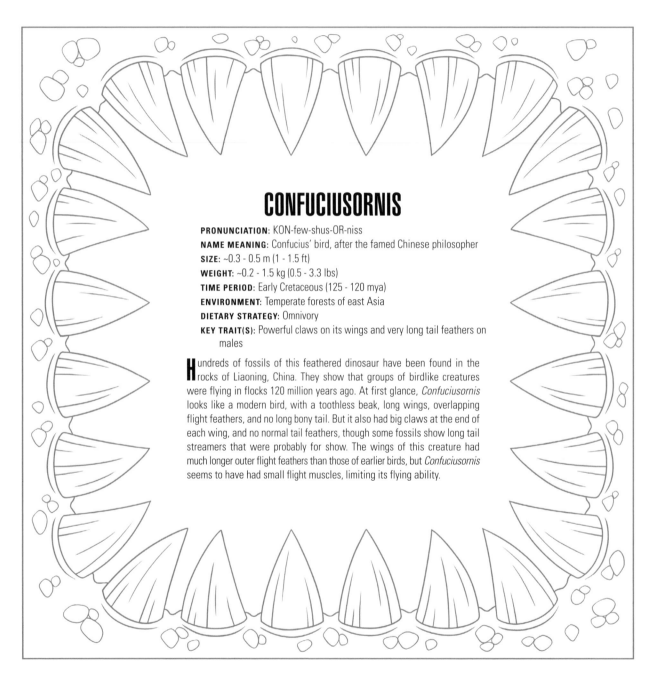

CONFUCIUSORNIS

PRONUNCIATION: KON-few-shus-OR-niss
NAME MEANING: Confucius' bird, after the famed Chinese philosopher
SIZE: ~0.3 - 0.5 m (1 - 1.5 ft)
WEIGHT: ~0.2 - 1.5 kg (0.5 - 3.3 lbs)
TIME PERIOD: Early Cretaceous (125 - 120 mya)
ENVIRONMENT: Temperate forests of east Asia
DIETARY STRATEGY: Omnivory
KEY TRAIT(S): Powerful claws on its wings and very long tail feathers on males

Hundreds of fossils of this feathered dinosaur have been found in the rocks of Liaoning, China. They show that groups of birdlike creatures were flying in flocks 120 million years ago. At first glance, *Confuciusornis* looks like a modern bird, with a toothless beak, long wings, overlapping flight feathers, and no long bony tail. But it also had big claws at the end of each wing, and no normal tail feathers, though some fossils show long tail streamers that were probably for show. The wings of this creature had much longer outer flight feathers than those of earlier birds, but *Confuciusornis* seems to have had small flight muscles, limiting its flying ability.

KENTROSAURUS

PRONUNCIATION: KEN-tro-SORE-us

NAME MEANING: Sharp point lizard

SIZE: ~5m (16 ft) long

WEIGHT: ~900 kg (2,000 lbs)

TIME PERIOD: Late Jurassic (152 mya)

ENVIRONMENT: Coastal forests of Africa

DIETARY STRATEGY: Herbivory

KEY TRAIT(S): Dorsal plates were bony osteoderms embedded in the skin, not attached to the skeleton.

The smaller relative of the famous *Stegosaurus*, this Late Jurassic dinosaur was even more spectacular, thanks to its dramatic double row of dorsal plates and long, sharp spines. *Kentrosaurus* was one of the spikiest of these stegosaurs. Long, sharp spines would have been a very effective defense, and its spiky tail was a formidable weapon against theropods like *Allosaurus*. The plates and spines were also very impressive display features.

SCELIDOSAURUS

PRONUNCIATION: skel-EE-doe-SORE-us

NAME MEANING: Rib lizard; the name was originally intended to mean "limb lizard," but confused the ancient Greek words for "limb" and "rib"

SIZE: ~3.5 - 4 m (12 - 13 ft) long

WEIGHT: ~270 kg (600 lbs)

TIME PERIOD: Early Jurassic (196.5 - 183 mya)

ENVIRONMENT: Forests of Europe and Asia

DIETARY STRATEGY: Herbivory

KEY TRAIT(S): Armored skin with rows of bony knobs sheathed in horny keratin that formed a tooth-breaking armor.

The chunky, four footed *Scelidosaurus* was a member of a group of dinosaurs called thyreophorans which were beaked plant eaters that developed tough, bony defenses against hungry, sharp-toothed predators. The *Scelidosaurus* had a spiky tail with sharp-edged bony plates that made it a useful defensive weapon. The hind feet had four long toes, each tipped with a tough, blunt claw. *Scelidosaurus*, like the later thyreophorans, had simple leaf-shaped teeth for chewing through tough plant material.

CITIPATI

PRONUNCIATION: CHIT-ee-puh-ti

NAME MEANING: Funeral pyre lord, named for a Tibetan legend of dancing skeletons in a fire

SIZE: ~2.5 - 2.9 m (8 - 9.5 ft) long

WEIGHT: ~75 - 83 kg (165 - 183 lbs)

TIME PERIOD: Late Cretaceous (84 - 75 mya)

ENVIRONMENT: Plains and deserts of central Asia

DIETARY STRATEGY: Omnivory

KEY TRAIT(S): Short skull with bony ridge supporting a crest of keratin

*C*itipati was a toothless, short beaked theropod adapted to live on a broad diet of small animals, eggs, fruits, seeds, and other food. It was closely related to birds and fierce predators such as *Velociraptor*. *Citipati* had arms fringed with long, vaned feathers similar to birds. It stood on strong hind legs, and had powerful feet with long, stout claws. *Citipati* had fluffy feathers covering its body, and laid large, elongated eggs for its offspring. Skeletons of *Citipati* are often found sitting on their nest, caring for the eggs.

ORNITHOMIMUS

PRONUNCIATION: ORN-ith-oh-MIME-us
NAME MEANING: Bird mimic, because of its birdlike affinities
SIZE: ~3 - 3.8 m (10 - 12 ft) long
WEIGHT: ~113 - 170 kg (250 - 370 lbs)
TIME PERIOD: Late Cretaceous (76.5 - 66.5 mya)
ENVIRONMENT: Subtropical floodplains of western North America
DIETARY STRATEGY: Omnivory
KEY TRAIT(S): Toothless, beaked skulls, feathered body

This feathery theropod was named in the late 19th century during the "Bone Wars"—the bitter fossil-hunting rivalry between Edward Cope and Othniel Charles Marsh. *Ornithomimus* had long hind-limbs ending in three strong toes and long, slender, feather-covered arms. It was very ostrich-like in appearance, and the length of the limb bones suggests that it was a very fast runner. Large eyes support the hypothesis that *Ornithomimus* may have been nocturnal.

CHINDESAURUS

PRONUNCIATION: CHIN-di-SORE-us

NAME MEANING: Ghost lizard, from the Navajo word "chindi"

SIZE: ~2 - 2.3 m (6.5 - 7.5 ft) long

WEIGHT: ~45 - 50 kg (100 - 110 lbs)

TIME PERIOD: Late Triassic (235 - 210 mya)

ENVIRONMENT: Floodplains and forests of western North America

DIETARY STRATEGY: Carnivory

KEY TRAIT(S): Long arms, boxy head

One of the most physiologically primitive saurischian (lizard-hipped) dinosaurs, *Chindesaurus* survived in a time when there were not many other dinosaurs to share its environment. It lived beside *Coelophysis*, and the two probably competed for prey. During the Triassic Period, numerous lakes and rivers dominated the forested landscape of the southwestern United States, where *Chindesaurus* made its home. These lakes and rivers were full of large, dangerous predators called phytosaurs, crocodile-like reptiles. *Chindesaurus* would have had to watch the water carefully when it came to drink to make sure it didn't get snatched by another, bigger predator.

VELOCIRAPTOR

PRONUNCIATION: veh-loss-ih-RAP-tor
NAME MEANING: Fast thief
SIZE: ~2 m (6.5 ft) long
WEIGHT: ~15 kg (33 lbs)
TIME PERIOD: Late Cretaceous (75 - 71 mya)
ENVIRONMENT: Scrublands and deserts of central Asia
DIETARY STRATEGY: Carnivory
KEY TRAIT(S): Large killing claw on the second toe, grasping hands, small size

*V*elociraptor was a small, fast, feathered, and fierce hunter with a long tail that helped it maintain balance when attacking or fighting. Standing upright on two legs, *Velociraptor* adults could run very fast. Small forearms made it impossible for the *Velociraptor* to fly even though it was part of the group that gave rise to birds. The *Velociraptor* was one of the smaller dromeosaurids—birdlike hunters that were armed with special, sharp claws on each foot. Located on the second toe, the 6.5 cm (2.5 in.) claw was held off the ground, which kept it sharp. It might have been used to pin down struggling prey, while the rest of the foot provided grip, or was used like a climbing hook, to mount the backs of larger prey. Below its upturned snout, the dinosaur's jaws were filled with more than 60 teeth.

Smithsonian
DINOSAURS
Coloring Book